Overeat

....

When Enough Isn't Enough

Michael R. Emlet

WWW.NEWGROWTHPRESS.COM

New Growth Press, Greensboro, NC 27404
Copyright © 2019 by Michael R. Emlet

Unless otherwise indicated, Scripture quotations are taken from *The Holy Bible, English Standard Version.* Copyright © 2000; 2001 by Crossway Bibles, a division of Good News Publishers. Used by permission. All rights reserved.

Scripture quotations marked NIV are taken from THE HOLY BIBLE, NEW INTERNATIONAL VERSION®, NIV® Copyright © 1973, 1978, 1984, 2011 by Biblica, Inc.® Used by permission. All rights reserved worldwide.

Cover Design: Faceout Books, faceoutstudio.com
Interior Typesetting and eBook: lparnellbookservices.com

ISBN: 978-1-64507-003-0 (Print)
ISBN: 978-1-64507-005-4 (eBook)

Library of Congress Cataloging-in-Publication Data

Names: Emlet, Michael R., author.Title: Overeating : when enough isn't enough / Michael R. Emlet.
Description: Greensboro, NC : New Growth Press, [2019] |
Identifiers: LCCN 2019017426 (print) | LCCN 2019021462 (ebook) | ISBN 9781645070054 () | ISBN 9781645070030 (pamphlet)
Subjects: LCSH: Food--Religious aspects--Christianity. | Food habits--Religious aspects--Christianity. | Food habits--Psychological aspects. | Food in the Bible. | Hyperphagia--Religious aspects--Christianity.
Classification: LCC BR115.N87 (ebook) | LCC BR115.N87 E45 2019 (print) | DDC
    241/.68--dc23
LC record available at https://lccn.loc.gov/2019017426

Printed in South Korea

27 26 25 24 23 22 21 20   2 3 4 5 6

"Enough is as good as a feast."
—MARY POPPINS[1]

The Struggle with Overeating

Here's a confession: I like to eat. Too much. You can't tell that just by looking at me (which is true for just about any person). But it's a fact. I have a pattern of going well beyond what my grandmother used to call "delightfully full." Throughout my life, I've always had a massive appetite. To complicate matters, my father owned the local corner grocery store when I was growing up. I remember coming home from school many days, grabbing a bag of potato chips and a candy bar, and sitting down to consume them along with a quart of milk. And then I would eat a full dinner two hours later. And a bedtime snack. (And my father wondered why he struggled to make a profit on the business!) I never met a second portion I didn't like. "All you can eat" buffets? Well, of course I get my money's worth! Does any of this sound familiar to you?

Now, for better *and* for worse, my body's metabolism was such that for years I simply didn't gain much weight despite these disordered eating habits. Regular exercise helped, too. So, while it was good that I was not experiencing obvious health consequences of my overeating, it was not good that I could hide from reality.

But then I reached my late forties. My metabolism slowed. Exercise became more sporadic. The pounds started to accumulate, slowly but surely. There were seasons of greater self-control, to be sure. But now in my late fifties, this is a struggle that continues to manifest itself in my life. Many times, if I don't self-consciously and prayerfully approach my meals, I will still overeat. Period.

If you're reading this, I'm assuming you struggle with overeating too. Or, you care about someone who is struggling and want to help. My plan in this minibook is to answer the following questions: Why do I overeat? What does the Bible have to say about this struggle? What practical steps can I take to battle against overeating? My ultimate goal is to point you to Jesus Christ, who is your hope and your help for this struggle.

Because disordered eating can manifest itself so differently in our lives, it's important to highlight what this resource will not directly address:

- *Bulimia nervosa, or binge-eating disorder* (as described by the DSM-5).[2] Both of these problems involve episodes of "binge eating," but this kind of overeating generally requires regular counseling and a medical evaluation, especially if purging is present. Nevertheless, much of what I say should be helpful if you struggle in these particular ways.
- *Obesity.* Overeating may or may not correlate with obesity. A person can have a significant problem with overeating and not be overweight, or vice versa. There are a host of genetic and environmental factors that contribute to obesity, with total caloric intake being only one of many.[3]
- *The science of overeating.* There is research on overeating and obesity that contributes to this discussion

but it will remain, for the most part, implicit in my remarks. My goal is not a scientific treatise but a practical, biblically focused guide.

- *A discussion of healthy vs. unhealthy foods.* The struggle with overeating goes beyond the nutritional quality of the food consumed. You can overeat donuts, or vegetable soup made from scratch. I want to move away from the idea of "good" and "bad" foods. My focus is particularly on the amount of food consumed, not on the type of food, although it is wise to minimize the intake of highly processed foods.

First and foremost, this resource is primarily about helping those who continue to eat at mealtimes when they know they've had enough and who find this to be a consistent pattern in their lives.

Why Do We Overeat?

This is often a complex question, with multiple factors to consider. We have to take into account not only that we are God's image-bearers who live in relationship to him, but also that we do this with our bodies! God created human beings as both body and spirit. Further, we live in dynamic relationship with other people, and in particular, situational and cultural contexts. So how does this factor into why we overeat? Perhaps we've skipped a meal and are feeling really hungry. Or, we are with a group of friends who generally overindulge during a given meal. Or, we are in a cultural context where our hosts offer course after course of food. Or, our parents consistently praised us for being members of the "clean plate club," and we remain happy to oblige. Or, there is an abundant supply of ready-made snack foods in our pantry.

But let me simplify a bit. While there may be many factors contributing to our tendency to overeat, I want to focus on what happens within us when we sit down to a meal and come away from it knowing that we've had too much. What's most important to see here is that overeating is not simply a behavioral or body issue but also a "heart" issue. In Scripture, the heart is used to describe our moral center, the reality that moment by moment our loves are directed either toward God or toward someone/something else (Romans 1:18–23).

Jesus, in explaining sin, points to the inside as the source of all attitudes and behavior: "But what comes out of the mouth proceeds from the heart, and this defiles a person. For out of the heart come evil thoughts, murder, adultery, sexual immorality, theft, false witness, slander. These are what defile a person" (Matthew 15:18–20a). Jesus could just have easily said, "For out of the heart comes overeating." The reasons why we overeat ultimately connect to our relationship with the living God. Put another way, food is a litmus test of our worship, showing what we most love, want, or fear in the moment. Appetites are not just physical; they have a spiritual character as well.

So, it's not enough to decide we have a problem with overeating. We need to ask *why*. We need to get to the spiritual heart of the matter. There are many heart-oriented reasons why we overeat.

Pleasure

Sometimes we overeat because we just don't want the wonderful multisensory experience of sight, smell, and taste of food to end. We enjoy a good thing too much. Enough is not enough, and we continue eating beyond the satisfaction of our hunger. Our want overrules our need. Sometimes a member of my family will ask me as I reach for another helping, "Do you really need that?" In other words, "Is your desire for more motivated by inordinate pleasure or by actual physical need at this point?"

But shouldn't we enjoy our food? Absolutely! After all, God gives "wine to gladden the heart of man, oil to make his face shine and bread to strengthen man's heart" (Psalm 104:15). Eating is more than a dutiful transaction to ingest raw calories!

But when pleasure becomes an end in itself, the internal cry for "more" trumps the sober realization that I've had enough. No doubt the drive for "more" is influenced by our western culture's preoccupation with "super-sizing" happiness at all costs. "Why should you deny yourself this pleasure?" the world whispers. Faced with a tasty and artfully prepared meal (or even a large order of fries) it's hard to resist overdoing it! But we don't want the pleasure of the gift to turn us away from the Giver.

Pain

Sometimes we overeat in response to negative emotions such as anxiety, sadness, guilt, or shame. Here, for a brief moment, we escape the negative emotions by virtue of the comfort, pleasure, and self-soothing afforded by food. The saying "drown your sorrows" should have a culinary equivalent! Sometimes we use food as a way to "fidget," to deal with fears and anxieties (although we might not be aware that we're using food this way!).

There's a reason why we use the term "comfort food." We can associate food with stress relief, peace, and happiness. "Hyperpalatable" foods (generally those high in sugar, salt, or fat) are especially good at this, since they tend to stimulate the brain's pleasure-reward pathway more strongly. But food can't ultimately bear the weight of our deep emotions. Rather, God invites us to bring our fears, frustrations, anger, disappointments, sadness, guilt, and shame to him—a practice seen repeatedly in the Psalms.[4]

Reward

Sometimes we overeat as a reward for good behavior. We come to a meal with a sense of entitlement: "I deserve to eat more at this meal since I watched myself carefully earlier today," or "I endured a hard day of work so I can indulge myself a bit." This results in viewing food in rigid, legalistic categories, rather than the God-oriented, relational ones I am proposing. In fact, the New Testament highlights that both overindulgent behavior and ascetic behavior have a law-like focus (i.e., break the rules or keep the rules), rather than a grace-based, relational focus (how can I honor Jesus who has bought me with his blood?).[5] With all of God's good gifts, we can swing from anxious abstinence to bold overindulgence. At either extreme, there is no sense of food as a gift from the Lord, to be enjoyed and stewarded well before him.

People-pleasing

While this may not be a consistent reason why we overeat, it's important to pay attention to settings where our overeating is connected with the expectations of others. If the people around you are eating too much, do you feel the pressure to conform by eating more than you need? Do you feel obligated to eat everything on your plate if someone else fixed it for you? How do you respond when someone exclaims, "Is that *all* you're eating?" At least consider if there are times when you overeat to fit in, to conform to the expectations of others.

Efficiency

Sometimes we overeat because we have a "bolt-and run" mentality. We have to get through this meal because there are important tasks to accomplish. Like the White Rabbit in Disney's version of *Alice in Wonderland,* we cry, "I'm late! I'm late! For a very important date! No time to say hello, goodbye! I'm late! I'm late! I'm late!"[6]

When we eat fast, we're likely to eat more, because there is a lag time between food entering our stomach and our sense of fullness. Perhaps you've had the experience of feeling comfortably full at the conclusion of a quickly eaten meal, only to feel uncomfortably stuffed fifteen minutes later. That's the problem with eating too fast—you get ahead of your own God-given physiological mechanisms to signal relief of hunger.

The bottom line in all these heart-oriented reasons for overeating is this: Instead of viewing food as nourishment from God, we use it to pursue pleasure, to prop up our emotions, to reward ourselves, and to fit in with a crowd. Food becomes a commodity to use (and abuse) to get what we want. It becomes something disconnected from the Giver of the gift.

I want to return to something I said at the beginning of this section. Having highlighted the importance of understanding the desires and fears active at the level of your motivations, don't overlook the many other factors that may contribute to a given episode of overeating. Those factors could include: unplanned skipping of a meal earlier in the day leading to excessive hunger, type of food present, where you're eating (home vs. restaurant), whether you're eating alone or with others, family of origin patterns of eating, cultural expectations, and time of day, to name a few. These bodily, relational, and social factors can reinforce the heart-oriented reasons for overeating emphasized here.

Does this feel overwhelming to you? That's certainly not my aim! While I do think it's helpful to identify the *why*s of your overeating as clearly as possible, you (and I) don't change simply because we know ourselves better. We need power and perspective from outside ourselves. We can change and grow because God has given us everything we need for life and godliness through Jesus Christ (2 Peter 1:3). Part of the change process is having our attitudes about food and eating reshaped and renewed by Scripture. When we grasp God's gracious design for food in our lives we become increasingly motivated and hopeful.

What Does the Bible Say about Food?[7]

You can't read the Bible without encountering references to food, meals, feasts, and fasting. Food is a central theme in Scripture, and is connected to the relationship between God and his people. In the opening chapters of the Bible, God gives the vegetation of the newly created earth as food to the first human beings (Genesis 1:29). It's a gardener's paradise! But a short time later, food (fruit from the forbidden tree) becomes the occasion of Adam and Eve's rebellion against God (Genesis 3:1–13). Food continues to have a prominent place in the way fallen humanity relates to God, particularly in the system of sacrifices and festivals God prescribed for Israel. Isn't it interesting that God instituted meals of remembrance—the Passover meal (in the Old Testament) and the Last Supper (in the New Testament)—to showcase his redemption?

The centrality of food in God's relationship with people doesn't mean that food is involved in our actual salvation—but it does mean that our use of food is not morally neutral. Eating food must have a Godward orientation and motivation. Our use of food is an expression of our worship. This is why Paul can say, "So, whether you eat or drink, or whatever you do, do all to the glory of God" (1 Corinthians 10:31). Reading this verse in the context of Paul's larger discussion of idolatry reminds us that food can be a doorway to righteousness (deepening relationship with God) or a doorway to unrighteousness (turning away from God).

So, what are some biblical themes regarding food that can provide a framework to guide you in your struggle with overeating?

Food as Fuel

Tim Chester rightly says, "Food is so much more than fuel."[8] But it's certainly not *less* than that. We are bodily creatures! We need nourishment. We need to eat to survive. When we overeat, it is an extension of a natural process. Sometimes it's hard to know when a natural desire becomes gluttonous (i.e., self-indulgent). I'm not advocating an over-the-top "did I have one too many bites?" analysis after every meal! Focus on the obvious—"I've finished my second plateful and I feel like I'm going to explode." You *know* when you've had more than you need to nourish your body.

Appreciating food as fuel is part of being "fearfully and wonderfully made" (Psalm 139:14). God designed us to experience hunger, signaling that it's time to replenish our bodies. Have you ever had such a busy day that you forgot to eat until hunger pangs caught your attention? This reality reminds us that we are dependent, bodily creatures called to steward our bodies for God's glory. Eating wisely is one way we glorify God with our bodies.

Food as Sacrament

Here I'm not thinking of "sacrament" in the formal way we understand baptism and the Lord's Supper, but rather, sacrament in an informal sense—food as a sign pointing beyond itself. Food is a physical reality that points to spiritual realities having to do with our relationship with God, both now and in the future. Food points beyond itself, just as marriage points beyond itself to the relationship between Christ and the church (Ephesians 5:21–33).

In one sense, every biblical theme I highlight below underscores that food is more than mere fuel, important as that is. Food is more than a physical substance to address a physical need. Food not only strengthens and nourishes our body; it also shapes our soul and strengthens our relationships. This sets us apart from animal instinct. I guarantee that my dog has a one-track, purely physical mindset as she inhales her dog food each evening!

Author and pastor Steve DeWitt reminds us, "Don't eat strawberry pie like an atheist!"[9] What does he mean? Physical experiences such as having a meal point us toward God. Earthly pleasures are meant to serve as signposts directing us toward the source of true pleasure, God himself. This perspective guards us against eating for pleasure as an end in itself.

It's no wonder that Scripture employs metaphors associated with eating to describe our relationship with God: "Oh, taste and see that the Lord is good!" (Psalm 34:8). "When your words came, I ate them. They were my joy and my heart's delight" (Jeremiah 15:16, NIV).

Finally, there is a way in which food signals our certain future with Jesus Christ. One way eating a meal can be an act of spiritual formation is to realize that our eating is a foretaste of the marriage supper of the Lamb

(Revelation 19:6–9). Your meals now are literal appetizers for the banquet to come! Viewing food sacramentally should encourage you to experience a meal not as an endpoint in itself, but as a stepping stone toward the God who loves you.

Food as Gift

The provision of food is one way God shows his fatherly care. Perhaps you grew up "saying grace" before meals. Using that terminology reminds those gathered around the table that what is set before them (although prepared by a human cook and supplied by money earned by a human worker) ultimately is a good and gracious provision from our heavenly Father. It is why we rightly pray, "Give us each day our daily bread" (Luke 11:3).

One of the most striking examples in Scripture of God providing this gift to his people in need is the story of manna in the wilderness (Exodus 16). Ultimately, the gift was meant to provoke greater yearning for the Giver: "And he humbled you and let you hunger and fed you with manna, which you did not know, nor did your fathers know, that he might make you know that man does not live by bread alone, but man lives by every word that comes from the mouth of the LORD" (Deuteronomy 8:3). Once God's people reached the Promised Land, the manna stopped because they now "ate of the produce of the land" (Joshua 5:12)—another gift they did not labor for. God's gift of manna culminates in Jesus Christ, the bread of life (John 6:22–59). Unlike the provision of manna, feeding on Jesus leads to eternal life (John 6:48–51).

Recognizing food as a tangible physical gift reminds us of God's many other gifts to us, chief of which is Jesus himself (Romans 8:32). We say "thank you" for our meal. And we say "thank you" for salvation through Jesus Christ.

Food as Fellowship[10]

Food in Scripture is tied to relationship. We see this in both a "vertical" sense (food as a connecting point between God and his people) and a "horizontal" sense (food as a connecting point between people). Let's look at each in turn.

In the Old Testament, we see food as a meeting point between God and his people embedded in the sacrificial system, especially the fellowship or peace offering (Leviticus 3; 7:11–36), which was divided between the priest and the one who offered the sacrifice. It was the closest one could come to having God over for dinner! In addition, the series of festivals prescribed by the Lord for Israel (Leviticus 23) connected food with worship of God. In the New Testament, the Lord's Supper is a means of grace, a way in which God truly nourishes us spiritually in relationship with him (Matthew 26:26–28; 1 Corinthians 10:16).

Food not only draws us closer to God but also to one another. One of the most important ways to care for one another in ancient cultures was to provide hospitality (food, shelter, rest) to others. Hospitality represents the bounty of God's provision to you, extended to others in love. The call to hospitality is woven throughout Scripture.[11]

Overlapping with the biblical theme of hospitality is the idea of table fellowship. In Jewish (and early Christian) culture, eating a meal with particular people communicated something about the social order. In an honor/shame culture a meal either reinforced social standing or disrupted it. (Consider the hot water Jesus got into by eating with "tax collectors and sinners"! Matthew 11:19; Mark 2:13–17). This was a critical issue in the early church—could Jewish Christians eat with Gentile Christians? Rather than food serving as a marker of division and difference, meals (especially the Lord's Supper) brought an opportunity for unity (Acts 10:1–11:18; 1 Corinthians 10:17, 12:13; Galatians 2:11–14).

Eating food highlights that you're more than an individual consumer of needed nutrition; you're a community participant. This also makes you more conscious of food and its consumption within an interconnected web of human relationships and societies. As I was writing this, I realized just how much of a luxury it is to overeat. My own overeating occurs in the context of white, western middle-class values and affluence. Overeating (in terms of sheer quantity) is generally only a problem of abundance and privilege. My gluttony humbles me all the more when set next to a refugee fleeing the violence in South Sudan who may not have eaten more than a small bowl of porridge today, if even that.

These biblical themes I've pointed out remind you that food is not "neutral." It is a gift of God to be stewarded well. A biblical perspective on food provides the reason and motivation to fight against a pattern of overeating. Without it, the battle becomes one of an individual's will over food, which can so easily turn legalistic and self-absorbed. Approaching food and eating with a God-honoring perspective frees you to enjoy food, but most importantly, to enjoy the Giver of your daily bread.

Now let's look at how these biblical perspectives and motivations actually shape the specific ways we engage the battle of overeating.

Winning the Food Fight

First and foremost, remember that if you have entrusted your life to Christ, your identity is grounded in him. This is critical! You may be experiencing shame or feelings of guilt over this struggle. You're frustrated with the lack of progress. But count on this: Your problem with overeating (or any other struggle in the Christian life) does not define you. Jesus Christ does (Romans 8:1; 2 Corinthians 5:17; Galatians 2:20)! The very fact that you see overeating as an issue of discipleship, and that you want to change, is a mark of the Spirit in your life. It *is* challenging to live increasingly out of your identity as a son or daughter of God, but begin the battle from that place of security.

As you seek to change your eating habits, pay attention to other bodily disciplines in your life, including physical exercise and sleep. These practices hang together, particularly the connection between physical exercise and self-controlled eating. It's harder to overeat when you're exercising regularly. A healthy mindset often leads to healthy choices.

What about the role of sleep? We know that insufficient sleep can disrupt hormones that control hunger and appetite.[12] Also, staying up late means that you consciously experience the start of hunger when you would normally be asleep. Going to bed too late may provide an opportunity to eat again.

Practical steps to take before eating:

- *Evaluate* why *you're most likely to overeat.* Using the list of reasons mentioned earlier, what, for you, are the main contributors to your overeating? Are there other factors unique to you? Knowing potential snares and temptations helps you to be more spiritually alert.

- *Consider* when *you're most likely to overeat.* Is it during a regular meal? During a snack later? Knowing helps you to be prayerfully proactive during that time, rather than "drifting" into the pattern unknowingly.

- *Gauge your level of hunger as you sit down to eat.* Ideally, you're hungry but not ravenous. If the latter is true, ask God to help you take steps to guard your intake during the meal (see below).

- *Assess your emotional state prior to eating.* This is especially important if negative emotions tend to fuel your overeating. On a particular day, you might pray something like this, "Father, you know my tendency to eat too much when I'm stressed out. I'm really worried about the presentation to my department tomorrow. Help me to rest in your care. Walk with me in the midst of my anxiety. Remind me of my security in you. Now, as I eat this food, help me to 'taste and see' that you are good."

- *When possible, eat with other people.* I'm more prone to overeat when I eat alone. If you're single and living alone, consider setting up a rotating communal dinner. When I was a single physician, I gathered with two of my practice associates who were also single, one to two times per week. Usually it was more spontaneous than preplanned, but consider what works best for you. If you're married, extend hospitality to those who may otherwise dine alone.
- *Make your overeating a regular prayer concern.* It's hard to persist in praying, even for issues that you care deeply about! Meditate on several of the Scriptures we looked at earlier, and pray that you would approach meals as a springboard for experiencing God's grace and mercy. Pray that you would enjoy food as a foretaste of feasting with him in the new heavens and earth. Ask others to pray with and for you.

Practical steps to take during eating:

- *Eat regularly.* Research suggests that eating irregularly may contribute to obesity.[13] And eating regularly prevents a swing from ravenous hunger to uncontrolled eating.
- *Don't eat in front of a screen.* This is why meals or snacking in front of the TV can get out of hand. You're not thinking about your meal (nor enjoying

it, for that matter). The latest episode of your favorite show becomes the main attraction and eating becomes a mindless tag-along. Sometimes I have found myself eating additional food in order to watch a few more minutes online!

- *Make a "thanksgiving sandwich."* Pause to give thanks as you sit down to eat *and* as you finish. Bracket your eating with the grateful reception of God's good gift. This keeps you mindful of the Provider of your meal.

- *Have a first-portion size that is fairly equivalent to what others are eating.* Sometimes in an effort to curb overeating, we start with a tiny portion that just begs a second helping. Portion size tools (for example, a measuring cup) may be helpful in some instances. In general, we overestimate portion sizes (and this, too, is influenced by culture).

- *After you prepare your plate, put food containers away before you eat.* I find that sometimes, I will continue to eat more potato chips with my sandwich at lunch if the chip bag remains beside me on the table.

- *Slow down and savor the flavors of the meal.* How can you do this?

  - Cut food into smaller pieces. Notice the various aspects of taste as you chew—salty, sweet, bitter, sour, and savory. This helps with deliberate eating that is mindful of the Lord, the true source of pleasure.
  - Put your utensils down between bites.

- Pace yourself to the slowest eater at the table. In the culinary equivalent of Aesop's fable "The Tortoise and the Hare," my mother is a tortoise par excellence! I know few people who enjoy their food as much as she does, even at age eighty-five! And somehow, she always has enough room for dessert!
- Drink plenty of water. Not only is this good for your level of hydration, but it also contributes to expanding your stomach.
- Enjoy the conversation. A meal is not the equivalent of a NASCAR pit stop to replenish bodily fuel as fast as possible. Rather, it's an opportunity for fellowship. It's not just about the food; it's about the people eating the food in community. Maturity in eating moves from a "me" mentality to a "we" mentality.
- Pay attention to how full you feel. Eating slowly helps you to keep pace with your body's cues regarding hunger and fullness, as mentioned earlier. End when "delightfully full" rather than stuffed. Remember the experiential time delay between bites of food and the sense of fullness, which is an argument for eating slowly.
- After you eat, consider whether the amount you ate was wise—but don't go crazy with overanalysis.

What should you do when you overeat anyhow? It's certainly going to happen! I want to return to where this section started: Righteousness is *not* ultimately measured by calorie counts! Your acceptance and identity are in Jesus Christ, with whom you are united. And that gives you confidence even in the midst of failure. Turn to Jesus and away from guilt and shame.

Avoid an all-or-nothing mentality. OK, so you overate at lunch. But you have another opportunity at dinner. Receive God's mercies fresh for the next meal or day.

I want to mention briefly how the spiritual discipline of fasting may help with overeating. In the Bible, we see a rhythm of both feasting and fasting. But a pattern of overeating cultivates a perpetual feasting mindset. When we proactively choose to fast, we are more mindful of God and our absolute dependency on him. We are less likely to take food for granted. Fasting accentuates food as a gift and keeps it from being too important in our lives.[14]

Lastly, see your doctor if you are unable to curb your overeating, particularly if obesity and other health issues such as diabetes and high blood pressure are developing. For some people, a consultation with a nutritionist can be helpful.

"Open Your Mouth and I Will Fill It!"

I want to conclude with the perspective gained from Psalm 81. This psalm begins with a call to feasting (vv. 1–4), tying it to God's redemption of Israel from Egypt (vv. 5–7). But it also provides a warning against idolatry. It is a plea for God's people to listen to him (vv. 8–9). Yet, pay attention to how God appeals to his people in verse 10: "I am the LORD your God, who brought you up out of the land of Egypt. Open your mouth wide and I will fill it." Wow, no stinginess here! He is the provider of all good things—our daily bread and ultimately, redemption through Jesus Christ, the Bread of Life (John 6:35).

Connecting the dots between food and our relationship with God and others is the foundation for change in the struggle with overeating. Our God stands ready to help you. By his grace, may you increasingly experience that "enough is as good as a feast."

Endnotes

1. Bill Walsh, Don DaGradi, and P. L. Travers. *Mary Poppins.* Motion picture. Directed by Robert Stevenson. Burbank, CA: Walt Disney Productions, 1964. I'm indebted to Jayne Clark for pointing me to this quote.

2. *Diagnostic and Statistical Manual of Mental Disorders*, 5th edition (DSM-5) (Washington, DC: American Psychiatric Association, 2013), 345–353.

3. For a concise overview, see Harvard Health Publishing, "Why People Become Overweight," Harvard Medical School, June 2009, accessed January 3, 2019, http://www.health.harvard.edu/staying-healthy/why-people-become-overweight.

4. For example, see Psalms 10, 13, 22, 56, 61, 77, 88, and 130.

5. See, for example, 1 Corinthians 6:12–20; Colossians 2:20–23; and 1 Timothy 4:4–5.

6. Lewis Carroll, Winston Hibler, et al. *Alice in Wonderland.* Motion picture. Directed by Clyde Geromini,

Wilfred Jackson, and Hamilton Luske. Burbank, CA: Walt Disney Productions, 1951.

7. A number of helpful resources explore the significance of food from a biblical perspective, including Tim Chester, *A Meal with Jesus: Discovering Grace, Community, and Mission around the Table* (Wheaton, IL: Crossway, 2011); Rachel Marie Stone, *Eat with Joy: Redeeming God's Gift of Food* (Downers Grove, IL: IVP, 2013); and Norman Wirzba, *Food and Faith: A Theology of Eating* (New York: Cambridge University Press, 2011).

8. Chester, *A Meal with Jesus,* 11.

9. Steve DeWitt, *Eyes Wide Open: Enjoying God in Everything* (Grand Rapids, MI: Credo House Publishers, 2012), 120.

10. Norman Wirzba, from the foreword to Stone, *Eat with Joy*, 9.

11. The examples of hospitality and the commands to care for one another using food and other material means are too numerous to mention, but include passages such as Ruth 2, Isaiah 58:6–7, Matthew 25:31–46, Romans 12:13, and 1 Peter 4:9.

12. Harvard Health Publishing, "Why People Become Overweight."

13. Ibid.

14. For a very helpful overview of the biblical rationale for fasting see Don Whitney, "9 Reasons to Fast Other Than 'It's Swimsuit Season,'" *Christianity.com*, July 27, 2011, accessed February 21, 2019, http:/www.christianity.com/bible/9-reasons-fast-other-than-swimsuit-season.html.